A Plan of Action

A Play

Philip Ayckbourn

A Samuel French Acting Edition

SAMUELFRENCH.COM
SAMUELFRENCH-LONDON.CO.UK

Copyright © 2008 by Philip Ayckbourn

All Rights Reserved

A PLAN OF ACTION is fully protected under the copyright laws of the United States of America, the British Commonwealth, including Canada, and all other countries of the Copyright Union. All rights, including professional and amateur stage productions, recitation, lecturing, public reading, motion picture, radio broadcasting, television and the rights of translation into foreign languages are strictly reserved.

ISBN 978-0-573-02384-2

www.SamuelFrench.com
www.SamuelFrench-London.co.uk

FOR PRODUCTION ENQUIRIES

UNITED STATES AND CANADA

Info@SamuelFrench.com

1-866-598-8449

UNITED KINGDOM AND EUROPE

Plays@SamuelFrench-London.co.uk

020-7255-4302/01

Each title is subject to availability from Samuel French, depending upon country of performance. Please be aware that A PLAN OF ACTION may not be licensed by Samuel French in your territory. Professional and amateur producers should contact the nearest Samuel French office or licensing partner to verify availability.

CAUTION: Professional and amateur producers are hereby warned that A PLAN OF ACTION is subject to a licensing fee. Publication of this play does not imply availability for performance. Both amateurs and professionals considering a production are strongly advised to apply to Samuel French before starting rehearsals, advertising, or booking a theatre. A licensing fee must be paid whether the title is presented for charity or gain and whether or not admission is charged. Professional/Stock licensing fees are quoted upon application to Samuel French.

No one shall make any changes in this title for the purpose of production. No part of this book may be reproduced, stored in a retrieval system, or transmitted in any form, by any means, now known or yet to be invented, including mechanical, electronic, photocopying, recording, videotaping, or otherwise, without the prior written permission of the publisher. No one shall upload this title, or part of this title, to any social media websites.

For all enquiries regarding motion picture, television, and other media rights, please contact Samuel French.

MUSIC USE NOTE

Licensees are solely responsible for obtaining formal written permission from copyright owners to use copyrighted music in the performance of this play and are strongly cautioned to do so. If no such permission is obtained by the licensee, then the licensee must use only original music that the licensee owns and controls. Licensees are solely responsible and liable for all music clearances and shall indemnify the copyright owners of the play(s) and their licensing agent, Samuel French, against any costs, expenses, losses and liabilities arising from the use of music by licensees. Please contact the appropriate music licensing authority in your territory for the rights to any incidental music.

IMPORTANT BILLING AND CREDIT REQUIREMENTS

If you have obtained performance rights to this title, please refer to your licensing agreement for important billing and credit requirements.

A PLAN OF ACTION

First performed by Quorum Theatre Company as part of a southern France schools tour 2008, with the following cast:

Roger Holmes	David Raymond
Samantha Shaw	Judi Armstrong
Liam Holmes	Gregory A. Smith
Tabitha Shaw	Becky George

Directed by Philip Ayckbourn
Designed by Lucy French

CHARACTERS

Roger Holmes, 40
Liam Holmes, Roger's 16-year-old son
Samantha Shaw, Roger's girlfriend, 40
Tabitha Shaw, Samantha's 16-year-old daughter

SYNOPSIS OF SCENES

The action of the play takes place in the respective living-rooms of Roger Holmes and Samantha Shaw.

SCENE 1	7.20 in the evening
SCENE 2	Ten minutes later
SCENE 3	7.00 the following evening
SCENE 4	9.00 the next morning
SCENE 5	10.00 that evening
SCENE 6	7.00 the following evening
SCENE 7	Two hours later
SCENE 8	9.00 the next morning
SCENE 9	7.30 that same evening
SCENE 10	9.00 the next morning
SCENE 11	2.00pm, a few days later
SCENE 12	7.30 that same evening

Time — the present

PRODUCTION NOTE

Scene change music should assist by being brief and punchy. This will help signify a passage of time whilst not overly interrupting the flow of the action.

A licence issued by Samuel French Ltd to perform this play does not include permission to use the Incidental music specified in this copy. Where the place of performance is already licensed by the PERFORMING RIGHT SOCIETY a return of the music used must be made to them. If the place of performance is not so licensed then application should be made to the Performing Right Society, 29 Berners Street, London W1T 3AB (website: www.mcps-prs-alliance.co.uk).

A separate and additional licence from PHONOGRAPHIC PERFORMANCES LTD, 1 Upper James Street, London W1R 3HG (website: www.ppluk.com) is needed whenever commercial recordings are used.

FIREARMS AND OTHER WEAPONS USED IN THEATRE PRODUCTIONS

With regards to the rules and regulations of firearms and other weapons used in theatre productions, we recommend you read the Entertainment Information Sheet No. 20 (Health and Safety Executive).

This information sheet is one of a series produced in consultation with the Joint Advisory Committee for Broadcasting and the Performing Arts. It gives guidance on the management of weapons that are part of a production, including firearms, replicas and deactivated weapons.

This sheet may be downloaded from: www.hse.gov.uk. Alternatively, you can contact HSE BOOKS, PO Box 1999, Sudbury, Suffolk, CO10 2WA Tel: 01787 881165 Fax: 01787 313995.

A PLAN OF ACTION

Scene 1

Roger Holmes' and Samantha Shaw's respective living-rooms. It is 7.20 p.m.

Although the action takes place more or less in the same stage space we are to believe it is taking place in separate rooms in separate houses. The invisible dividing wall between the two rooms is often quite flexible but generally SR *is the Holmes' residence and* SL *is the Shaws' residence*

There is a lounge, a chair, a mirror, and a framed photo of Roger's late wife SR. *There are also some lockable french windows.* SL *there is a lounge, a mirror and a hi-fi stereo with a remote control*

When the Lights come up Tabitha is seated SL *reading a book and Liam is seated* SR *playing a hand-held computer game*

Samantha enters SL

Samantha Well? (*She goes to the mirror and checks her appearance*) Maybe the skirt's better. What do you think? Tabby?
Tabitha Whatever, Mum. I don't care.
Samantha I do. I want your advice. Aren't you going to make an effort, put something nice on?
Tabitha What for?
Samantha For him.
Tabitha No, why should I?
Samantha To make a good impression.
Tabitha I don't want to make a good impression.
Samantha Please yourself.
Tabitha I will.

Samantha exits SL

Roger enters SR

Roger OK, Liam, nearly ready are you?
Liam No.

Roger goes to the mirror and checks his appearance

　　Look, can't I just stay here and watch TV?
Roger　No.
Liam　I don't want to spend my evening with some girl I don't even know.
Roger　You'll need to meet her sometime.
Liam　Why?
Roger　She's pretty.
Liam　I don't care. She's that woman's daughter.
Roger　That "woman" has a name you know. Samantha.
Liam　Poor Mum, if she could see you now.
Roger　She'd be happy; happy that I've found love again.
Liam　No she wouldn't, she'd be devastated.
Roger　Please, Liam, we're going to be late.
Liam　This is murder.

Liam exits SR

Roger dials his mobile. Samantha's mobile rings

Tabitha　(*calling off*) Mum, phone.
Samantha　(*off*) Can you answer it please?

Tabitha looks at the display screen on the phone

Tabitha　(*calling off*) It's him.
Samantha　(*off*) Answer it.

Tabitha answers the mobile phone

Tabitha　(*into Samantha's mobile*) Hallo?
Roger　(*into his mobile*) Hallo my sexy love bunny ... Hallo?
Tabitha　(*into Samantha's mobile*) It's Tabitha.
Roger　(*into his mobile*) Oh ... Hallo Tabby. How are you?
Tabitha　(*into Samantha's mobile*) OK.

Samantha enters SL. *She takes the mobile from Tabitha*

Samantha　(*into her mobile*) Hallo.
Roger　(*into his mobile*) Hallo. How's my sexy love bunny?
Samantha　(*into her mobile*) She's fine. Looking forward to seeing her gorgeous huggly bear.

Scene 2

Tabitha Ugh!

Tabitha exits SL

Roger (*into his mobile*) I've booked the restaurant for eight.
Samantha (*into her mobile*) Lovely.
Roger (*into his mobile*) We're just leaving — hopefully. Be with you in ten.
Samantha (*into her mobile*) How's Liam?
Roger (*into his mobile*) Fine. Tabitha?
Samantha (*into her mobile*) OK. It'll be good for them to have this evening together.
Roger (*into his mobile*) Yes. I'm sure they'll like each other, eventually.
Samantha (*into her mobile*) I'm sure.
Roger (*into his mobile*) Well, see you soon. Kiss, kiss.
Samantha (*into her mobile*) Kiss, kiss, kiss.
Roger (*into his mobile*) Kiss, kiss, kiss, kiss.

They hang up

(*Calling off*) Liam, we're going. Now!

Roger exits SR

Samantha checks her appearance in the mirror

Samantha Oh ... no.

Scene change music plays

Samantha exits SL

Scene 2

Ten minutes later

Tabitha enters SL *and sits in the lounge, reading a magazine*

The doorbell rings

Tabitha (*calling off*) Mum, he's here. Mum? Oh.

Tabitha exits SL

Roger (*off*) Hallo, Tabitha.

Tabitha enters followed by Roger

Tabitha She's upstairs changing. Again.
Roger (*calling off*) Liam?

Liam enters SL

Liam, this is Tabitha.
Tabitha Hi.
Liam All right.
Roger OK ... Ah, yes.

Roger takes out his wallet

For food.

He gives a note to Liam

Samantha enters SL

Ah ha, here she is.
Samantha Here I am.
Roger And doesn't she look delicious?
Samantha Why thank you, kind sir.

Samantha and Roger kiss

Hallo, Liam.
Liam Hi.
Samantha Right. Plenty to eat in the fridge, darling.
Roger All taken care of.
Samantha Ah. Well, have fun you two.
Roger See you, Liam.
Samantha Bye, sweetie.

Roger and Samantha exit SL

There is a pause

Scene 2

Tabitha So ...
Liam So ... I didn't want to come, you know.
Tabitha I didn't want you to come.
Liam He forced me to.
Tabitha This is very awkward.
Liam We don't have to talk. I can just watch TV.

There is a pause

Tabitha Mum, she's not even divorced yet. It's hardly been four months since she and Dad split up.
Liam It's only been a year since my mum died.
Tabitha No offence, but your dad doesn't compare to my dad, no way.
Liam Well your mum doesn't compare to my mum. No offence.
Tabitha Well ...
Liam Well ...

There is a slight pause

Tabitha You are allowed to take off your coat, if you want.

There is a slight pause

   So... Drink?
Liam What have you got?
Tabitha What do you want?
Liam Beer.
Tabitha No beer.
Liam Wine?
Tabitha Ah ... no.
Liam Anything alcoholic?
Tabitha Sherry.
Liam Oh God, this is what hell is like.
Tabitha We could buy some beer and pizza. Watch a movie.
Liam Got anything good?
Tabitha That depends on what you mean by good.
Liam Action films, sci-fi, horror?
Tabitha No.
Liam Didn't think so.
Tabitha We could rent something, something we both want to watch.
Liam That might be difficult.
Tabitha I'm sure we could find something.

Liam OK. But remember, just because we're doing this, it doesn't mean we're friends or ever going to be friends, is that understood?
Tabitha Don't worry.
Liam We're just making the best of a bad situation.
Tabitha I agree.
Liam OK.
Tabitha OK. Let's go.

Scene change music plays

   They exit SL

SCENE 3

The following evening, 7.00 p.m.

Roger enters SR, *carrying a sealed envelope and talking on his mobile phone*

Roger (*into his mobile*) Right, I'll meet you at the theatre then shall I? ... Right. ... Yes. Kiss, kiss.

   Samantha enters SL

Samantha (*into her mobile*) Kiss, kiss, kiss.
Roger (*into his mobile*) Kiss, kiss, kiss, kiss.

They hang up. Samantha checks her appearance in the mirror

   (*Calling off*) Liam I'm going. There's a letter for you. By hand. I'll leave it here shall I? Liam? Ah.

   Roger puts the envelope in an obvious place and exits SR

   Tabitha enters SL, *carrying a book*

Samantha You'll be all right then, will you? Oh, smile, darling. You should be pleased for me. I'm happy again. Roger's a good man. He's a good man and a kind man.
Tabitha Yes, but he's not Dad, is he?
Samantha No ... he's not Dad. Oh, I'm going to be late. How do I look? Right, I'll see you later, sweetie.

   Samantha exits SL

Scene 3

Liam enters SR *and notices the letter. He opens the envelope and reads it*

Tabitha exits SL

Liam dials his mobile. Tabitha's mobile rings

Tabitha enters carrying a bag and answers her mobile

Tabitha (*into her mobile*) Hallo?
Liam (*into his mobile*) Hi, it's me, Liam.
Tabitha (*into her mobile*) Hi. You got my letter?
Liam (*into his mobile*) Yes, obviously. What do you want to speak to me about?
Tabitha (*into her mobile*) I've got an idea.
Liam (*into his mobile*) An idea?
Tabitha (*into her mobile*) Yes.
Liam (*into his mobile*) For what?
Tabitha (*into her mobile*) Look, can you come over, it's difficult to explain over the phone.

Liam sighs

It's in your interest too.
Liam (*into his mobile*) All right. This better be good.
Tabitha (*into her mobile*) Can you come now?
Liam (*into his mobile*) Yes.

They both hang up

Liam exits SR

Tabitha puts on some make-up. She then takes a wig from her bag and puts it on. She removes her casual top revealing something more provocative beneath. She examines herself in the mirror

Tabitha Oh ... glasses.

She takes a pair of designer glasses from her bag and puts them on, then strikes poses before the mirror

Hallo, I'm Cynthia. No — more exotic. Hi, I am Chiquita. No — too exotic. Something in between. Hallo, I am ... Sophie ... Sophie from Paris ... *oui*. 'Ello *monsieur*. I am very pleased to meet you, *monsieur*.

The doorbell rings. Tabitha takes off her wig and glasses and puts them back in the bag. She puts her top back on

Tabitha exits SL *with the bag*

Liam enters SL *followed by Tabitha, who is no longer carrying the bag*

Liam So what's your big idea then?
Tabitha I'll tell you. Drink? I've got beer.

Tabitha exits SL

Liam takes out his mobile and attends to a text message

After a few moments Tabitha enters, carrying the bag and some shoes, unseen by Liam. She is now wearing a provocative outfit and wears the wig and glasses. She puts her shoes on quietly

(*In a French accent*) Bonjour, *monsieur*.
Liam Oh ... Hallo.
Tabitha (*in a French accent*) 'Ave you seen Tabby?
Liam Yes she's in ...
Tabitha (*in a French accent*) I am Sophie, a friend. I am staying here.
Liam Ah.
Tabitha (*in a French accent*) You are?
Liam Liam.
Tabitha (*in a French accent*) Her boyfriend, perhaps?
Liam No.
Tabitha (*in a French accent*) Do you have a girlfriend, Liam?
Liam Er, no.
Tabitha (*in a French accent*) Good. I am looking for a boyfriend for me.
Liam Ah ...
Tabitha (*in a French accent*) But perhaps you do not like girls, *monsieur*.
Liam Yeah.

Tabitha starts to laugh. She removes the wig and glasses

Scene 3

Tabitha Fooled you.
Liam What!
Tabitha Well?
Liam What are you doing?
Tabitha (*in a French accent*) I am being Sophie.
Liam Why are you being Sophie?
Tabitha It's my disguise. All part of our plan. What do you think?
Liam What plan?
Tabitha To stop my mum and your dad from being together.
Liam Huh?
Tabitha You introduce me to your dad as your new French friend, Sophie. And I introduce you to my mum as my new Italian friend.(*She pulls out another wig from her bag*) Giuseppe. Mum likes Italian men. Do you think your dad will find me sexy as Sophie?
Liam Wait, wait, wait, wait, wait. Explain.
Tabitha I am going to seduce your dad as Sophie and you are going to seduce my mum as Giuseppe.
Liam Oh no.
Tabitha Oh yes.
Liam You are not serious.
Tabitha I am. Look, all we need to do is get them interested in us. We don't have to do anything, just promise things. And then we agree to meet them secretly, alone. Arrange it for them to be "accidentally" discovered — you know, by each other. Their deceit is exposed. They fight, they part, Sophie and Giuseppe mysteriously disappear. Mission accomplished. Simple.
Liam Oh, simple. You don't think they might recognize us?
Tabitha You didn't recognize me.
Liam Yeah, maybe, but they're in love aren't they — perfectly happy together thank you.
Tabitha People can be tempted.
Liam No. It's a stupid idea.
Tabitha OK, then there's obviously nothing we can do. My mum and your dad will stay together. They'll get married, possibly have more children. All of us: one big happy family. If that's what you want.
Liam Of course it's not what I want.
Tabitha Then let's do something to stop it.
Liam There has to be a better way than this.
Tabitha Well, I'm listening.

There is a pause

Liam What if they discover it's us?

Tabitha They won't, not if we're careful — and believable.

There is a slight pause. Tabitha holds out Liam's wig

   Giuseppe?
Liam How can I be Italian? I don't speak Italian. That's not believable for a start.
Tabitha Neither does Mum. Does your dad speak French?
Liam No.
Tabitha Perfect.

There is a slight pause

   Go on.
Liam This is crazy, crazy. (*He takes the wig and puts it on*)
Tabitha Not bad. OK, tell me your name.
Liam Giovanni.
Tabitha Giuseppe.
Liam Whatever. Giuseppe.
Tabitha You're Italian.
Liam (*with an Italian accent*) Giuseppe.
Tabitha Better. (*With a French accent*) So, *monsieur*, you are Giuseppe? *Si.*
Liam (*with an Italian accent*) *Si.*
Tabitha (*with a French accent*) I am Sophie. *Enchanté monsieur.* (*She holds out her hand*) Kiss my hand.

Liam kisses Tabitha's hand

   More passion. Like an Italian man would.

Liam kisses Tabitha's hand more passionately

   (*With a French accent*) Oh, *monsieur*! Do you find me sexy, *monsieur*?
Liam (*with an Italian accent*) No.
Tabitha *Si*, you do. (*with an Italian accent*) *Si*, I do, *signorina*.
Liam (*with an Italian accent*) *Si*, I do, *signorina*.
Tabitha That's better. (*With a French accent*) I think Italian men are very sexy *monsieur*. Speak words of love to me. Tell me how beautiful I am.

Scene 3

There is a slight pause

(*With an Italian accent*) You are very beautiful, *signorina*.
Liam (*with an Italian accent*) You are very beautiful, *signorina*.
Tabitha (*with a French accent*) Ah *oui*?
Liam (*with an Italian accent*) *Si*.
Tabitha More. (*With an Italian accent*) You have beautiful eyes.
Liam (*with an Italian accent*) You have beautiful eyes.
Tabitha (*with a French accent*) Ah *oui*?
Liam (*with an Italian accent*) *Si* and ...

Tabitha grins

A beautiful smile, *signorina*.
Tabitha (*with a French accent*) Ah *oui*? Hold me in your arms, *monsieur*. (*In her usual voice*) Well go on.

Liam holds Tabitha in his arms

Tighter. That's better. (*With a French accent*) Kiss me. (*In her usual voice*) Kiss my neck.

Liam kisses her neck

With passion. Think Italian.

Liam accidentally stands on Tabitha's foot

Ow!
Liam (*casting off his wig*) This is crazy. It will never work.
Tabitha Ah! You just need some practise that's all. I need to teach you how to seduce a woman — without standing on her foot. Let's have something to eat. We'll practise again later. Come on.

Tabitha picks up Liam's wig, her book and her bag and exits SL, *limping*

Liam What am I doing? What am I doing?

Scene change music plays

Liam exits SL

Scene 4

The following morning, 9.00 a.m.

Roger enters SR

Roger (*into his mobile*) I'm sorry, darling. I can't see you tonight ... Liam wants me to meet a friend of his ... A girl.

Samantha enters SL

Samantha (*into her mobile*) Oh, I see.
Roger (*into his mobile*) Sophie I think her name is. He does seem keen that I should meet her for some reason. It's funny, he's usually quite secretive about his girlfriends.
Samantha (*into her mobile*) It may be serious.
Roger (*into his mobile*) That'll be a first.
Samantha (*into her mobile*) Well ...

Tabitha enters SL, carrying her handbag

Roger (*into his mobile*) Tomorrow?
Samantha (*into her mobile*) OK, tomorrow then. What shall we do?
Tabitha Remember, Mum, Giuseppe tomorrow evening.
Samantha Oh, oh yes.
Roger (*into his mobile*) What's that?
Samantha (*into her mobile*) No, tomorrow evening Tabby wants me to meet someone.
Roger (*into his mobile*) Oh.
Samantha (*into her mobile*) A new friend, coming to dinner.

Liam enters SR

Roger (*into his mobile*) I see. Well, Friday then. (*To Liam*) Bye, Liam, see you this evening.
Liam Bye, Dad.

Roger exits SR

Samantha (*into her mobile*) Look I'd better go, I'm going to be late... Yes, OK... Kiss, kiss, kiss. (*She hangs up. To Tabitha*) OK darling I'm off. See you later.
Tabitha Remember I'm seeing Rachel this evening, Mum.

Scene 5

Samantha Right, well, have fun. Bye.
Tabitha Bye.

Samantha exits SL

Tabitha dials her mobile. Liam's mobile rings and he answers it

Liam (*into his mobile*) Hallo?
Tabitha (*into her mobile*) It's me. All set?
Liam (*into his mobile*) Yeah. I said you'd be here for seven-thirty.
Tabitha (*into her mobile*) Right.
Liam (*into his mobile*) Look …
Tabitha (*into her mobile*) What?
Liam (*into his mobile*) Just be convincing, all right?
Tabitha (*into her mobile*) Don't worry, I will. See you tonight.

They hang up. Liam considers what he is doing

Tabitha notices the photo of her dad in her bag. She takes it out and looks at it. She dials her mobile

(*Into her mobile*) Hey Dad, it's Tabby … No I just wanted to say hi that's all … Yeah … Yeah …

Tabitha exits SL

Liam picks up the photo of his mum

Liam I'm doing this for you, Mum. Tell me if you disapprove. Mum?

He looks up in the room waiting for a sign

OK then.

Scene change music plays

Liam exits SR

Scene 5

That evening, 10.00 p.m.

Samantha enters SL *with a hot drink. She sits, bored*

Tabitha (*as Sophie; off*) So I said to him "you English are so crazy".

Tabitha and Roger laugh off stage R

Roger (*off*) Very good, very good.
Tabitha (*as Sophie; off*) Crazy people.
Roger (*off*) Quite right too, quite right, we are.

There is more laughter off stage R

Samantha dials her mobile

Samantha (*into her mobile*) Hallo darling ... Yes OK. How's your evening going?

Roger enters SR with his mobile and a glass of wine

Roger (*into his mobile*) Fun. So far so good.
Samantha (*into her mobile*) Ah.
Roger (*into his mobile*) Everything all right?
Samantha (*into her mobile*) Yes. So what's she like, this Sophie?
Roger (*into her mobile*) Nice girl. Seems friendly.
Samantha (*into her mobile*) That's good.
Roger (*into his mobile*) What are you doing?
Samantha (*into her mobile*) Oh, nothing really.
Roger (*into his mobile*) Ah.
Samantha (*into her mobile*) Well, don't let me keep you from your guest. I just wanted to say hallo.
Roger (*into his mobile*) I'll call you tomorrow, darling.
Samantha (*into her mobile*) OK.
Roger (*into his mobile*) Kiss, kiss.

Roger hangs up

Samantha (*into her mobile*) Kiss, kiss ... kiss.

Samantha hangs up and exits SL

Roger goes to the mirror and checks his appearance

Tabitha enters SR. She is disguised as Sophie and carries a wine glass and her bag

Tabitha (*as Sophie*) Knock knock. Excusez-moi.

Scene 5

Roger Come in, come in, please.
Tabitha (*as Sophie*) Thanks. You have a nice house, Roger.
Roger Thank you.
Tabitha (*as Sophie*) Very comfortable.

There is a slight pause

Roger Is Liam ...?
Tabitha (*as Sophie*) Ah, Liam has gone to bed.
Roger To bed!
Tabitha (*as Sophie*) Yes, he had a little ... how do you say — *mal de tête*?
Roger Headache?
Tabitha (*as Sophie*) Yes, that's it, headache.
Roger Oh. He seemed OK a moment ago.
Tabitha (*as Sophie*) Very sudden. Perhaps you would like me to go home. If it is uncomfortable for —
Roger No, oh no, no, I'm happy — if you ...
Tabitha (*as Sophie*) I am happy, *monsieur*. It is not often I get to talk to a gentleman Englishman like yourself.
Roger And it's not often I get to talk to a pretty young French mademoiselle like yourself.
Tabitha (*as Sophie*) Oh.
Roger So, you met Liam at a party you say?
Tabitha (*as Sophie*) *Oui, monsieur*.
Roger Are you and Liam ...?
Tabitha (*as Sophie*) *Monsieur*?
Roger You know ... in love?
Tabitha (*as Sophie*) *Non, monsieur*, he is nice but he is too young for me.
Roger Oh.
Tabitha (*as Sophie*) My preference is for the older man.
Roger Ah. How old are you Sophie, if you don't mind me asking?
Tabitha (*as Sophie*) I am nineteen, *monsieur*.
Roger Oh, I thought you were younger, more Liam's age.
Tabitha (*as Sophie*) No *monsieur*, nineteen.
Roger So school is finished for you?
Tabitha (*as Sophie*) All finished.
Roger University?
Tabitha (*as Sophie*) *Non*, I want to follow my career.
Roger Oh and what's that?
Tabitha (*as Sophie*) Singing, *monsieur*.
Roger Singing. Opera?

Tabitha (*as Sophie*) Cabaret.
Roger Ah.
Tabitha (*as Sophie*) Clubs, bars, you know.
Roger Locally?
Tabitha (*as Sophie*) Here and there. I follow the money.
Roger Well, I must come and see you sometime.
Tabitha (*as Sophie*) You must. I would like that, Roger. (*She indicates the photo of Roger's late wife*) Your wife, Roger?
Roger Yes.
Tabitha (*as Sophie*) She was very beautiful.
Roger Yes.
Tabitha (*as Sophie*) You are in love again, perhaps with someone else?
Roger Well ...
Tabitha (*as Sophie*) *Non*?
Roger Love, what is love?
Tabitha (*as Sophie*) Love is when two people cannot resist one another, when all they want is to hold that other person, to kiss that other person, to make love to that other person ... I think.
Roger Yes, so do I.
Tabitha (*as Sophie*) Have you ever loved a French woman, Roger?
Roger No, no I haven't.
Tabitha (*as Sophie*) Ah, a pity. We are very passionate lovers, *monsieur*.
Roger Ah.
Tabitha (*as Sophie*) Have you ever kissed a French woman, Roger?
Roger No, no.
Tabitha (*as Sophie*) We are very passionate kissers, *monsieur*.
Roger Oh, really?
Tabitha (*as Sophie*) Yes. I'm sorry, perhaps I should go. I am making you feel —
Roger No, not at all, I'm very ... Please stay, please — Drink your wine.
Tabitha (*as Sophie*) Well, only if you are happy?
Roger Yes I'm happy. Very happy.
Tabitha (*as Sophie*) So am I.
Roger Good, then we are both happy.
Tabitha (*as Sophie*) Yes, both happy. (*Indicating her wine*) Sorry, *monsieur*, perhaps it is this that is making me ...
Roger Yes?
Tabitha (*as Sophie*) Making me ...
Roger Yes?
Tabitha (*as Sophie*) Want to ...

Scene 6

Roger Want to?
Tabitha (*as Sophie*) Want to …
Roger Yes?
Tabitha (*as Sophie*) Want to …
Roger Yes?
Tabitha (*as Sophie*) To …
Roger Yes?

They are about to kiss but Tabitha stops his mouth with her hand

Tabitha (*as Sophie*) Forgive me, *monsieur*.
Roger No, forgive me please, I'm … sorry I ——
Tabitha (*as Sophie*) … Do not be sorry, *monsieur*. I must go.
Roger Yes, of course.

Tabitha takes a notepad and pen from her bag. She writes her number and gives it to Roger

Tabitha (*as Sophie*) My phone number, Roger.
Roger Your number!
Tabitha (*as Sophie*) If you perhaps want to … maybe …
Roger Ah.
Tabitha (*as Sophie*) Without … (*Indicating Liam*) If you wish.
Roger Ah…
Tabitha (*as Sophie*) *Allez*, thank you for a very pleasant evening, Roger. I will see myself out, *monsieur*. À la prochaine, peut-être. [*Until the next time, perhaps*]
Roger Yes.
Tabitha (*as Sophie*) *Bonsoir*.
Roger *Bonsoir*.

Tabitha exits SR

Roger considers what he is doing. Scene change music plays

Roger exits SR

SCENE 6

The next day, 7.00 p.m.

Samantha enters SL. *She takes her make-up from her bag and puts some on*

Liam enters SR

Liam (*calling off*) Dad? Dad?

Liam dials his mobile

    (*Into his mobile*) Hi, it's me. ... Yeah, I'm just leaving. ... He's happy. You did well it seems. ... Oh. ... I don't know, I just — with your mother. ... I know. ... Yes. ... Yes I know, OK. ... I will, I am.

Roger enters SR

    Oh hi Dad. (*Into his mobile*) I'll see you later, George, bye. (*He hangs up*)

Roger You look smart.
Liam Good evening last night?
Roger Yes it was, yes.
Liam Better go.
Roger Have fun.
Liam Yes.

Liam exits SR

Roger takes out Sophie's number. He picks up his mobile and considers

Roger Hallo Sophie, it's me, Roger. Hallo Sophie, it's Roger. Hi beautiful, it's me Roger. French, French, a bit of French. *Bonjour ... Ça va? C'est moi. Bonjour, c'est moi Roger, ça va?* Perhaps, Sophie, this evening we could —

His mobile rings

    (*Answering his mobile*) Hallo? ... Sophie! I was just thinking about you... Yes? ... How did you get my number? ... Yes, of course. Listen Sophie, tonight if you're ... (*Deflated*) Ah. ... I see. ... Yes. ... (*Inspired*) Oh, yes. ... Well, all right then. ... Yes. ... *Au revoir.*

He hangs up then considers for a moment before exiting SR

Samantha goes to the mirror and checks her appearance. She looks at her watch

Samantha He's late.

Scene 6

The doorbell rings

After a few moments Tabitha enters SL *with Liam who is disguised as Giuseppe*

Tabitha Mum, this is Giuseppe.
Samantha Hallo, Giuseppe.
Liam (*as Giuseppe*) *Signora*, it is a pleasure.

Liam kisses Samantha's hand

Samantha Ah. A pleasure to meet you too, Giuseppe.
Liam (*as Giuseppe*) You have a beautiful house, *signora*.
Samantha Oh, thank you.
Liam (*as Giuseppe*) In Italy we say "beautiful houses are made by beautiful women".
Samantha Do you?
Liam (*as Giuseppe*) *Si, signora*. It is a joy to be here.
Samantha Samantha please. Now let's see if I remember. *Buona sera. Come stai?* [*Good evening. How are you?*]
Liam (*as Giuseppe; laughing nervously*) *Buona sera. Come stai?*
Samantha *Bene, grazie, signore. E tu?* [*Good, thank you, sir. And you?*]
Liam (*clapping his hands; as Giuseppe*) Ah ... Tabitha said you spoke no Italian, *Signora*.
Samantha *Un poco*. [*A little*]
Tabitha That's enough of that, Mum. Don't embarrass yourself — and me.
Samantha A drink, Giuseppe? Some wine, perhaps?
Liam (*as Giuseppe*) As you wish, *signora*.
Samantha Come through.

Samantha exits SL

Tabitha Don't worry, that's all the Italian she knows, I promise. You look good. OK?
Liam (*as Giuseppe*) No.
Tabitha Confidence. After you, Giuseppe.

Scene change music plays

Liam exits SL, *followed by Tabitha*

Scene 7

Two hours later

Roger enters SR *with a glass of wine and a French phrase book. He turns to various pages as he cobbles together his speech*

Roger (*reading from the book*) *Bonjour. Heureux de vous revoir mademoiselle. Entrez, je vous prie. Asseyez-vous. Un verre de quelque chose? De vin, peut-être? Je ne serai pas long. Mettez-vous à l'aise.* (*Repeating the phrases from memory*) *Bonjour. Heureux de vous revoir mademoiselle. Entrez, je vous prie. Asseyez-vous. Un verre de quelque chose? De vin, peut-être? Je ne serai pas long. Mettez-vous à l'aise.* [*Hallo. Pleased to meet you again miss. Enter please. Sit down. Drink? Wine perhaps. I won't be a minute. Make yourself comfortable*] (*He finishes his wine and flips through the phrase book. Reading*) *Encore du vin.*

Roger exits SR

Samantha enters SL, *finishing off a glass of wine*

Samantha Come through, come through.

Liam and Tabitha enter SL

Well, we are having fun, aren't we?
Tabitha Yes, Mum.
Liam (*as Giuseppe*) *Si, signora.* Much fun.
Samantha Ah ... Another drink Giuseppe?
Liam (*as Giuseppe*) No, no, thank you, no.
Tabitha I know, let's have some music.
Samantha Good idea.
Tabitha Mum loves to dance, don't you, Mum?
Samantha Oh.
Tabitha So does Giuseppe, eh Giuseppe?
Liam (*as Giuseppe*) *Si?*
Tabitha *Si.*
Samantha *Si?*
Liam (*as Giuseppe*) *Si.*
Tabitha You should both have a little dance together.
Samantha What does Giuseppe have to say?
Liam (*as Giuseppe*) *Si* ... I love to dance.

Scene 7

Tabitha See. Something appropriate.

Tabitha takes the remote control and turns on the hi-fi stereo. She selects a station. Music plays

That will do.

Samantha starts to dance. Tabitha nudges Liam into action and then takes out her mobile

I need to give Rachel a call.
Samantha OK, darling.

Tabitha gestures for Liam to hold Samantha. Liam does so

Oh.

Tabitha exits SL

After a few moments Liam tentatively places a hand on Samantha's bottom. Samantha removes it. They continue to dance. Liam pulls away

Liam (*as Giuseppe*) I am sorry, *signora*. (*He turns off the stereo*)
Samantha Sorry?
Liam (*as Giuseppe*) Si, *signora*.
Samantha For what?
Liam (*as Giuseppe*) It is difficult for me, *signora*.
Samantha Difficult?
Liam (*as Giuseppe*) Si, to dance when my heart is — Oh, *signora*!
Samantha What is it? Are you in pain?
Liam (*as Giuseppe*) Si, *signora*, great pain.
Samantha Do you have a heart problem?
Liam (*as Giuseppe*) Si, *signora*.
Samantha Shall I call a doctor?
Liam (*as Giuseppe*) No, *signora*, it is not medical. It is a pain of desire.
Samantha Desire?
Liam (*as Giuseppe*) Si, *signora*.
Samantha Desire for what?
Liam (*as Giuseppe*) For you, *signora*.
Samantha For me?
Liam (*as Giuseppe*) Si, *signora*.
Samantha But Giuseppe ——

Liam (*as Giuseppe*) ... Oh, *signora*, forgive me, *signora*, I am sorry. I am ashamed. But I cannot stop my heart. I do not want to stop my heart. When I look at you, when I hold this ... kiss this hand.
Samantha Giuseppe!
Liam (*as Giuseppe*) Shame, *signora*, such shame. Forgive me, forgive me. *Signora*, you are so beautiful.
Samantha You're very sweet Giuseppe but ——
Liam (*as Giuseppe*) ... Yes I know, I know, you feel nothing for me, *signora*, nothing?
Samantha I do, of course, yes but ...
Liam (*as Giuseppe*) You love another.
Samantha Well, yes ... I ... I ... Giuseppe ——
Liam (*as Giuseppe*) ... Don't touch me, *signora*, please. It is too much. (*Pause*) Touch me, *signora*.
Samantha Giuseppe!
Liam (*as Giuseppe*) Oh have pity on me, *signora* Samantha. I cannot fight my desire when I look upon such beauty. I am helpless, helpless, helpless!
Samantha Giuseppe please, Tabitha.
Liam (*as Giuseppe*) Tabitha! Tabitha! I'm in love with your mother!
Samantha Shh, Giuseppe please.
Liam (*as Giuseppe*) I will not "shh", I want to tell the whole world!
Samantha Giuseppe.
Liam (*as Giuseppe*) The whole world, *signora*, must hear me!

Tabitha enters SL

Samantha Tabitha.
Tabitha What's happening? Giuseppe?
Samantha Giuseppe. Tabitha's here.
Tabitha Giuseppe?
Liam (*as Giuseppe; composing himself*) Forgive me. I must go. *Signora*. Tabitha.

Liam exits SL

Samantha Well.
Tabitha What was that all about, Mum?
Samantha I don't know.
Tabitha Goodness. Ha!
Samantha Yes, indeed, goodness me.
Tabitha So ...
Samantha Hmm?

Scene 8

Tabitha Well …?
Samantha Well what?
Tabitha Nothing … just …
Samantha Yes?
Tabitha What do you think?
Samantha About what?
Tabitha Giuseppe. He's fit.
Samantha What are you suggesting?
Tabitha No harm in a little bit of fun.
Samantha Who for?
Tabitha For you.
Samantha Me!
Tabitha I'm just saying ——
Samantha No. Anyway aren't you jealous? He is your friend.
Tabitha Yeah, but not my boyfriend. I don't love him so …
Samantha Enough! Well, an interesting evening nevertheless. Perhaps a little more wine I think, to calm things down.

Samantha exits SL

Tabitha Hmm.

Scene change music plays

Tabitha exits SL

SCENE 8

The following morning, 9.00 a.m.

Roger enters SR. *He goes to the mirror and ties his tie*

Roger Bonjour. Heureux de vous revoir, mademoiselle. Entrez, je vous prie. Asseyez-vous. Un verre de quelque chose? De vin, peut-être? Je ne serai pas long. Mettez-vous à l'aise. (*He considers for a moment and then dials his mobile phone. Into his mobile*) Hallo, darling. How are you? … Ah …

Tabitha enters with her book SL

Oh dear. Take a pill … Yes, I'm just leaving. Look, tonight I ——

Samantha enters in her dressing gown SL

Samantha (*into her mobile*) ... Yes, I think I might have a quiet evening in tonight, if you don't mind.
Roger (*into his mobile*) Oh?
Samantha (*into her mobile*) Sorry to be boring.
Roger (*into his mobile*) Oh, no ... no.
Samantha (*into her mobile*) More energy for the weekend.
Roger (*into his mobile*) Yes, absolutely.
Samantha (*into her mobile*) What were you going to say?
Roger (*into his mobile*) Oh, nothing. The weekend then. Better dash.
Samantha (*into her mobile*) OK darling. Kiss, kiss.
Roger (*into his mobile*) Kiss, kiss.

They hang up

Roger exits SR

Tabitha Morning, Mum. Headache? Too much wine.
Samantha Coffee.

Samantha exits SL

Tabitha dials her mobile phone

Tabitha (*into her mobile*) Hi, it's me ... Yeah, you did well. She liked you but ... it's going to be difficult.

Liam enters SR

Liam (*into his mobile*) What do we do now?
Tabitha (*into her mobile*) We need to concentrate on your dad.
Liam (*into his mobile*) Oh.
Tabitha (*into her mobile*) Look, we've started this so we have to continue. We can't stop now. OK? (*Short pause*) OK?
Liam (*into his mobile*) OK.
Tabitha (*into her mobile*) Mum's staying at home tonight which means your dad's free to see me. You have to tell him that you're staying the night with a friend so you'll be out of the way. Yes?
Liam (*into his mobile*) Yes.
Tabitha (*into her mobile*) We'll discuss details later.

Roger enters SR *with a cup of coffee*

Scene 8

Liam (*into his mobile*) OK, Steve, I'll see you later then. Bye. (*He hangs up*) OK, Dad?
Roger Liam.
Liam Oh, I'm staying at Steve's tonight, Dad.
Roger Oh, are you. All night?
Liam All night. Is that OK?
Roger Yes ... fine. Why shouldn't it be?

Liam exits SR

Roger takes out his mobile and considers a moment

Samantha enters SL *holding a cup of coffee*

Samantha I'm going to lie down for a while. I'll go to work later.
Tabitha OK, Mum.

Samantha exits SL

Roger (*calling off*) Liam? Liam?

Roger dials his mobile. Tabitha's other mobile rings. She answers it

Tabitha (*as Sophie; into her mobile*) 'Ello?
Roger (*into his mobile*) Sophie, it's me Roger.
Tabitha (*as Sophie; into her mobile*) Oh, Roger. How are you?
Roger (*into his mobile*) Good.
Tabitha (*as Sophie; into her mobile*) Good.
Roger (*into his mobile*) And you?
Tabitha (*as Sophie; into her mobile*) *Bien.*
Roger (*into his mobile*) Good. Ah, are you free tonight for dinner at my place, perhaps?
Tabitha (*as Sophie; into her mobile*) Oh yes, Roger. I would like that very much.
Roger (*into his mobile*) Yes?
Tabitha (*as Sophie; into her mobile*) *Oui,* Roger. What about Liam?
Roger (*into his mobile*) He's staying the night with a friend.
Tabitha (*as Sophie; into her mobile*) I see.
Roger (*into his mobile*) So, we can be alone.
Tabitha (*as Sophie; into her mobile*) Yes.
Roger (*into his mobile*) Shall we say seven-thirty?
Tabitha (*as Sophie; into her mobile*) Seven-thirty.
Roger (*into his mobile*) Right, well, see you later, Sophie.

Tabitha (*as Sophie; into her mobile*) *Oui*, Roger, later. *Au revoir*.
Roger (*into his mobile*) *Au revoir*.

They hang up. Roger looks at his watch

Oh God.

He hurriedly exits SR

Tabitha OK. New outfit.

Scene change music plays

Tabitha exits SL

Scene 9

That evening, 7.30 p.m.

Liam, disguised as Giuseppe, appears outside the french windows, carrying a sword. He dials his mobile

Liam (*into his mobile*) Hi, it's me ... Yes, I am. Have you left yet? ... OK ... Yes ... OK. (*He hangs up and looks through the windows*)

Roger enters SR *with a glass of wine. He sings the first few lines of "Chanson d'amour" then checks his appearance in the mirror*

Roger *Ton parfum est la senteur du paradis.* [*Your perfume has the scent of paradise*] *Je suis perdu dans tes yeux.* [*I am lost in your eyes*] *Ton parfum est la* ——

Liam accidentally knocks his sword against the windows. Roger goes to investigate and Liam hides. Roger opens the windows

Hallo? Anyone here? Sophie? Hallo?

Roger closes the windows. Liam surfaces from his place of hiding

Roger exits SR

Tabitha, disguised as Sophie, enters outside the SR *windows, carrying a bottle of wine*

Scene 9

Tabitha Hey.
Liam Oh! God, don't do that.
Tabitha Sorry. What's that for?
Liam Self defence. Just in case. It's OK.
Tabitha Yours?
Liam No. When do I call your mum?
Tabitha Better do it now.

Tabitha hands Liam the second mobile phone from her pocket

Use this one. Secret number. You know what to say?
Liam Yes. (*He takes the mobile and dials. Into the mobile*) Hallo, *signora*? ... Yes, it is me, Giuseppe. ... I need to tell you something, *signora* ... Listen to me, *signora*. ... Your man Roger, he is false, false. He is a liar and a cheat. ... I know this. Believe me, *signora*, I say this because I love you. ... *Signora*, please. Tonight he is with a woman. ... *Signora*, listen to me, a young woman. ... In his house. I am outside, watching. He is full of lies. ... Come and see for yourself, *signora*, if you do not believe me. Come now, *signora*. *Signora*? *Signora*? (*He hangs up*)

Tabitha Is she coming?
Liam I don't know. What do we do?
Tabitha Hope for the best.

Tabitha exits SR

Samantha enters SL. *She ponders. She is about to dial her mobile but changes her mind. She exits* SL

Tabitha enters the living-room SR

After a few moments Roger enters SR *with another glass of wine which he gives to Tabitha*

Roger Du vin.
Tabitha (*as Sophie*) Merci.
Roger Avec plaisir. Santé. [*With pleasure. Good health.*]
Tabitha (*as Sophie*) Santé.
Roger You are looking very beautiful, Sophie.
Tabitha (*as Sophie*) Merci, Roger. Do you like the wine?
Roger Yes, lovely.
Tabitha (*as Sophie*) It is from the Loire Valley.

Roger Beautiful.
Tabitha (*as Sophie*) Do you have a favourite wine, Roger?
Roger What colour are your eyes, Sophie? Blue?
Tabitha (*as Sophie*) Blue-green I think. A red, or a white perhaps?
Roger Yes, blue-green. Lovely.
Tabitha (*as Sophie*) You notice the good aromas.
Roger I do. And lovely skin too.
Tabitha (*as Sophie*) Hmm?

Roger strokes Tabitha's arm. Tabitha pulls away

Roger Is everything all right?
Tabitha (*as Sophie*) Yes. *La nuit est encore jeune.* The night is young.
Roger Ah, yes.
Tabitha (*as Sophie*) *Lentement.* (*Slowly*) It is more enjoyable *lentement.* Let us talk about you: your work at the bank.
Roger I'd rather not. Let's talk about you: about France, your homeland.
Tabitha (*as Sophie*) No, *monsieur*, not that.
Roger No?
Tabitha (*as Sophie*) It is unhappy memories for me.
Roger Ah, oh dear. Well, something pleasant ... your music then.
Tabitha (*as Sophie*) My music?
Roger Yes, your cabaret.
Tabitha (*as Sophie*) Ah ...
Roger I know.
Tabitha (*as Sophie*) What?
Roger Why don't you sing me a song?
Tabitha (*as Sophie*) A song!
Roger Yes.
Tabitha (*as Sophie*) You do not want to hear me sing, Roger.
Roger But I do, I do.
Tabitha (*as Sophie*) No.
Roger Yes. Sing me ... I know, what's that one from the musical? You must know it: "Willkommen, Bienvenue", yes?
Tabitha (*as Sophie*) Yes I, of course. One of my favourites.
Roger Mine too. Pretend this is your club — or "Chez Roger's". Let me relieve you of that.

Roger takes Tabitha's wine glass

Tabitha (*as Sophie*) Really, Roger I ——

Scene 9

Roger Come on, Mademoiselle Sophie. I've paid good money to see you. Entertain me.

Tabitha sings the first verse of "Willkommen, Bienvenue" and Roger joins in at the end

Roger Wonderful, wonderful!
Tabitha (*as Sophie*) Thank you Roger, it is better with the music, of course.
Roger I should imagine you are very popular. You are even more beautiful when you sing — if that's possible. I must kiss you.
Tabitha (*as Sophie*) I ——
Roger I must.
Tabitha (*as Sophie*) Later.
Roger Now. *Mon coeur est enflammé.* [*My heart is on fire*]
Tabitha (*as Sophie*) Pardon?
Roger *Mon coeur est enflammé.*
Tabitha (*as Sophie*) Ah ...
Roger You want to kiss me, don't you?
Tabitha (*as Sophie*) Yes I do but ——
Roger Then why wait? Let us kiss, now!

The doorbell rings

Tabitha (*as Sophie*) Who's that?
Roger I don't know.
Tabitha (*as Sophie*) Are you expecting someone, Roger?
Roger No. Liam perhaps. Damn! Better hide. Outside, through the windows. Here take your glass.
Tabitha (*as Sophie*) But Roger ——
Roger Hurry.

Liam hides as Roger hurries Tabitha through the windows

Just wait there.
Tabitha (*as Sophie*) Roger ——
Roger Shhh!

Roger closes the windows. He tidies himself and exits SR

Tabitha Pssst? Liam?
Liam Here.

Tabitha Is that her?
Liam Yes.
Tabitha Good. He's locked me out.
Liam Don't worry I know a trick. I do it all the time. (*He manages to free the lock*) There.

Samantha enters SR, *followed by Roger*

Samantha So, you're alone then, are you?
Roger Yes, just me.
Samantha I smell perfume.
Roger I don't smell anything.
Samantha Definitely perfume.
Roger Oh must be that — what's her name ... Sophie.
Samantha Sophie?
Roger Yes, she was here with Liam. Left about half an hour ago. Must be hers. It's not mine.
Samantha Ah.
Roger Is something the matter?
Samantha No. It's nothing. The silly man.
Roger Man? What man?
Samantha Oh no-one. Well, since I'm here, perhaps a little glass of something.
Roger Absolutely. *Vin rouge*?
Samantha Sure.

Roger exits SR

Tabitha OK, give me a few moments, then come in.
Liam Wait.

Liam takes Tabitha's glass and takes a large swig. He passes it back to Tabitha. She enters through the windows. Liam steps back so Samantha cannot see him

Tabitha (*as Sophie*) Who are you?
Samantha Who are you?
Tabitha (*as Sophie*) I am Sophie.
Samantha Oh. And where's Liam?
Tabitha (*as Sophie*) I do not know.
Samantha Isn't he with you?
Tabitha (*as Sophie*) No, I am not with him.
Samantha No?

Scene 9

Tabitha (*as Sophie*) No. So who are you?
Samantha I am Samantha, Roger's girlfriend.
Tabitha (*as Sophie*) Roger did not mention you.
Samantha No, I'm sure he didn't.

Roger enters with a glass of wine

Roger Here we are darling — Ah! Sophie! What are you doing back — without Liam?
Samantha It's all right, she's explained everything.
Roger Has she?
Samantha Yes.
Roger Ah well, that's ... good.
Samantha Is it.
Roger Isn't it?
Samantha No. So you're having a wonderful time with your little French tart, are you?
Roger Ah, listen Samantha ——
Samantha Get away from me you despicable man. You unfaithful, false, beast of a man.
Roger Samantha please, I can explain. It's ——
Samantha Don't talk to me, don't ... Oh you ... you ... you ... you ——

Liam enters the living-room through the windows

Liam (*as Giuseppe*) *Signora*!
Samantha Giuseppe!
Roger What's this?
Liam (*as Giuseppe*) Forgive me, *Signora* Samantha, I could not restrain myself. My jealous heart makes me full of rage.
Roger Who are you?
Liam (*as Giuseppe*) I am Giuseppe.
Roger Do you know this boy?
Samantha I ——
Liam (*as Giuseppe*) ... Boy! I am a man, *signor*. See, see how false he is? He plays with this girl, this whore of his.
Tabitha (*as Sophie*) I am not a whore.
Liam (*as Giuseppe*) Whore. I would never be unfaithful to you, *Signora* Samantha. Never!
Samantha Giuseppe! Stop this!
Roger So, what have we here then? A young lover, perhaps?

Samantha Oh don't you try to —
Liam (*as Giuseppe*) Yes, I love her and I am ten times the man you are, *signor*. Twenty times!
Roger Get out of my house.
Liam (*as Giuseppe*) I take no orders from you, *signor*!

Liam holds the sword to Roger

Roger Now, now!
Samantha Giuseppe!
Liam (*as Giuseppe*) Perhaps I should avenge her honour, *signor*.
Roger Stay away from me, stay away.
Liam (*as Giuseppe*) Avenge! Avenge!
Samantha Giuseppe!
Liam (*as Giuseppe*) Stand still, *signor*.
Roger Help me someone, help! Help!

Roger runs off SR

Liam (*as Giuseppe*) Come back *signor*! *Signor*!

Liam chases him off SR

Roger (*off*) Help!
Samantha Giuseppe! We must call the police.
Tabitha (*as Sophie*) Pfff!
Samantha You, you — Ah!

Samantha exits SR

A few moments later Tabitha finishes her wine and exits SR

Roger appears outside the SR *windows. He is out of breath. He looks back to check that he's not been followed*

Roger (*looking through the windows; to himself*) Oh God! Oh God! You fool! You bloody fool!

Scene change music plays

Roger enters through the SR *windows then exits* SR

Scene 10

The following morning, 9.00 a.m.

Liam enters SR, *assisting Roger*

Liam Come on, Dad, walk, walk. That's it. Now sit. Oh.

Liam helps Roger into a chair

Roger She's gone, she's gone. It's all over. Finished. Finished.
Liam I'll make you some coffee.
Roger No coffee, no coffee. Whisky.
Liam I think you've had quite enough whisky, Dad. Coffee.

Liam exits SR

Samantha enters SL. *She sits and thinks*

Samantha The swine, the swine. (*Pause*) The swine!
Roger Oh.

Tabitha enters SL

Tabitha Do you want some tea?

Samantha nods

Tabitha exits SL

Liam enters SR *with a cup of coffee*

Liam Coffee, Dad.
Roger (*getting up*) I'm going to bed.
Liam Here ——
Roger No, no, I can manage.

Roger exits SR

Liam takes out his phone. He considers for a moment, then exits SR

Tabitha enters SL *with a cup of tea*

Tabitha Here you are, Mum.
Samantha I'm going out.
Tabitha Where to?
Samantha To the cinema.
Tabitha What are you going to see?
Samantha God knows.

Samantha exits SL

Tabitha dials her mobile

Tabitha (*into her mobile*) Hi Liam, it's me. ... Oh are you? ... Sure. ... Yeah it's safe. ... All right, see you soon. (*She hangs up. She considers for a moment and dials her mobile. Into her mobile*) Hi Dad, it's Tabby. ... Yeah I'm good. How are you? ... No, she's out. ... The cinema. ... I don't know. I'm seeing you tomorrow, yeah? ... Oh. ... Ah. ... No. ... It's OK, Dad. Have a good time. ... Yeah. Next weekend then. ... OK. ... Bye, Dad. ... Bye. (*She hangs up and considers for a few moments*)

The doorbell rings

Tabitha exits SL

After a moment she enters followed by Liam, who is carrying a bag

Liam So...
Tabitha Success.
Liam Success.
Tabitha How's your dad?
Liam Depressed. What about your mum?
Tabitha Depressed.

There is a slight pause

Liam Well, that's it.
Tabitha Yes, that's it.

There is a slight pause

Liam Here's your stuff.

There is a slight pause

Scene 10

Tabitha All for the best.
Liam Yeah.

There is a slight pause

Liam So, we'll never have to see each other ever again.
Tabitha No.
Liam Except in the street perhaps, the supermarket. We don't have to talk.
Tabitha No.

There is a slight pause

Liam Well.
Tabitha Well then.

There is a slight pause

Liam You did good, as Sophie.
Tabitha Thanks. You did good too, as Giuseppe. Very convincing.
Liam Thanks. You were, you know ...
Tabitha What?
Liam Well, quite ... sexy.
Tabitha Thanks. So were you.

There is a slight pause

Liam So ...
Tabitha So ...
Liam OK ...
Tabitha OK ...
Liam OK ...
Tabitha OK ...
Liam OK ...
Tabitha OK ...

They kiss

What are we doing?
Liam I don't know.

They kiss again

Tabitha Oh God, what have we done? Poor Mum.
Liam Poor Dad.
Tabitha We've been terrible. We've destroyed their lives. They loved each other.
Liam Yes, they did.

They kiss again

Tabitha I feel terrible.
Liam So do I.

They kiss again

I think I love you.
Tabitha I think I love you.

They kiss again

We must do something to help them.
Liam What?

Liam is about to kiss Tabitha again but she stops him

Tabitha We need to think.
Liam Yes.
Tabitha Come on.
Liam Where?
Tabitha My room.
Liam Yes?
Tabitha To think.
Liam Yes.
Tabitha Come on.

Scene change music plays

They exit SL

Scene 11

A few days later, 2.00 p.m.

Roger enters SR *with a crossword puzzle book. He sits and stares at the book*

Scene 11

Samantha enters SL *with a magazine. She sits and stares at it*

Roger takes out his mobile and considers a moment. Samantha takes out her mobile and considers a moment. Roger puts his mobile away and returns to his book. Samantha puts her mobile away and returns to her magazine

Liam enters SR

Liam Hi Dad?
Roger Oh, hallo Liam.

Tabitha enters SL

Tabitha Hi Mum?
Samantha Oh, hi Tabby.

Liam points to a clue in Roger's book

Liam Alaska.
Roger Ah.

Tabitha points to a picture in Samantha's magazine

Tabitha That's nice.

There is a pause

Liam Guess what, Dad? I saw Tabitha in the street today. You know —

Roger Yes, did you?
Liam She's actually quite ... OK.
Roger Hmm.
Tabitha Guess what, Mum? I saw Liam in the street today.
Samantha Ah.
Tabitha I was talking to him. He's actually quite ... friendly really.
Samantha Good.
Liam You know, Dad, she said her mum's really depressed.
Roger Is she?
Liam Yeah. She says she wants to call you but , you know, it's difficult, she's ... you know.
Tabitha He says his dad's very depressed, Mum. He really misses you, apparently.
Samantha Well.
Liam Perhaps you should call her, Dad. If you still love her.

Tabitha Why not call him, Mum. You love him.
Liam I'd better go. I've got football.
Roger Right.
Liam See you later.
Roger Yes.

Liam exits SR

Tabitha I said I'd meet Rachel. I'm late.
Samantha Right.
Tabitha Better go.
Samantha Yes.

Tabitha exits SL

Roger considers. He dials his mobile. Samantha's mobile rings. She looks at the display. She hesitates and then answers it

Samantha (*into her mobile*) Hallo.
Roger (*into his mobile*) Hallo.

There is a slight pause

 Look, I ...
Samantha (*into her mobile*) Yes?
Roger (*into his mobile*) I ... I ... I ...
Samantha (*into her mobile*) Yes?
Roger (*into his mobile*) How are you?
Samantha (*into her mobile*) Fine. You?
Roger (*into his mobile*) Er, fine.
Samantha (*into her mobile*) Right. We're both fine.
Roger (*into his mobile*) Ah, I was wondering if you, if we could ...
Samantha (*into her mobile*) Yes?
Roger (*into his mobile*) Talk.
Samantha (*into her mobile*) Talk?
Roger (*into his mobile*) Talk. (*Pause*) Hallo?
Samantha (*into her mobile*) Yes.
Roger (*into his mobile*) I'm very, very, deeply ...
Samantha (*into her mobile*) Yes.
Roger (*into his mobile*) Sorry.
Samantha (*into her mobile*) Yes, I ... Yes.

There is a slight pause

Roger (*into his mobile*) Perhaps tonight we could ...
Samantha (*into her mobile*) Tonight?
Roger (*into his mobile*) Or ...
Samantha (*into her mobile*) Tonight, yes.
Roger (*into his mobile*) Good. Good. Um ... Yours?
Samantha (*into her mobile*) Seven-thirty?
Roger (*into his mobile*) Seven-thirty.
Samantha (*into her mobile*) Right.
Roger (*into his mobile*) Right. Later then.
Samantha (*into her mobile*) Yes.
Roger (*into his mobile*) Bye then.
Samantha (*into her mobile*) Yes.

They both hang up. Scene change music plays

Roger exits SR

Samantha exits SL

Scene 12

That evening, 7.30 p.m.

Tabitha enters SR

A moment later Liam enters SR

Liam Sorry, no beer.
Tabitha Oh.

Liam holds Tabitha

Liam I'll have to make it up to you in some other way.

They kiss

Tabitha So this is it, you're officially my boyfriend?
Liam Yes I am, ma'am, officially your boyfriend, ma'am.
Tabitha And this is officially our first date?
Liam Yes it is, ma'am, officially —
Tabitha Oh, stop it.

They kiss

Samantha enters SL *holding flowers, followed by Roger*

Samantha They're lovely. Thanks.
Roger So, shall we talk?
Samantha Over dinner.
Roger OK.
Tabitha Let's go and eat.
Liam Later.
Tabitha Now. I'm hungry.
Liam So am I.
Tabitha For food.
Roger Where shall we go?
Tabitha I feel like pizza.
Samantha The pizza place?
Liam Good with me — if it's good with you.

Liam and Tabitha kiss

Roger Our first date. Remember?
Samantha Yes.

Roger kisses Samantha

Liam Come on then.
Samantha Come on then.

Liam takes Tabitha's hand. Roger takes Samantha's hand

They all exit

The Lights fade

CURTAIN

FURNITURE AND PROPERTY LIST

Scene 1

On stage: Lounge, chair, framed photograph of **Roger**'s late wife, french windows, mirror SR
Lounge, mirror, hi-fi stereo with remote control, **Samantha**'s mobile phone SL

Off stage: Book (**Tabitha**)
Hand-held computer game (**Liam**)

Personal: **Roger**: mobile phone (use throughout)

Scene 2

Off stage: Magazine (**Tabitha**)

Personal: **Roger**: wallet containing money

Scene 3

Off stage: Sealed envelope containing a letter (**Roger**)
Book (**Tabitha**)
Bag containing make-up, two wigs, glasses (**Tabitha**)
Shoes (**Tabitha**)

Personal: **Tabitha**: mobile phone (use throughout)
Liam: mobile phone (use throughout)

Scene 4

Off stage: Bag containing a photo of her dad (**Tabitha**)

Scene 5

Off stage: Hot drink (**Samantha**)
Glass of wine (**Roger**)
Glass of wine, bag containing a notepad and pen (**Tabitha**)

Scene 6

Off stage: Bag containing make-up (**Samantha**)

Personal: **Tabitha**: watch
Roger: Sophie's phone number

SCENE 7

Off stage: Glass of wine, French phrase book **(Roger)**
Glass of wine **(Samantha)**

SCENE 8

Off stage: Book **(Tabitha)**
Cup of coffee **(Roger)**
Cup of coffee **(Samantha)**

Personal: **Roger**: watch
Tabitha: second mobile phone

SCENE 9

Off stage: Sword **(Liam)**
Glass of wine **(Roger)**
Bottle of wine **(Tabitha)**
Glass of wine **(Roger)**
Glass of wine **(Roger)**

SCENE 10

Off stage: Cup of coffee **(Liam)**
Cup of tea **(Tabitha)**
Bag **(Liam)**

SCENE 11

Off stage: Crossword puzzle book **(Roger)**
Magazine **(Samantha)**

SCENE 12

Off stage: Flowers **(Samantha)**

LIGHTING PLOT

To open: Interior lighting

Cue 1   They all exit (Page 40)
         Lights fade

EFFECTS PLOT

Cue 1	**Roger** dials his mobile **Samantha**'s *mobile rings*	(Page 2)
Cue 2	**Samantha**: "Oh … no." *Scene change music*	(Page 3)
Cue 3	**Tabitha** enters SL and sits in the lounge, reading *Doorbell rings*	(Page 3)
Cue 4	**Tabitha**: "OK. Let's go." *Scene change music*	(Page 6)
Cue 5	**Liam** dials his mobile **Tabitha**'s *mobile rings*	(Page 7)
Cue 6	**Tabitha**: "I am very pleased to meet you, *Monsieur*." *Doorbell rings*	(Page 8)
Cue 7	**Liam**: "What am I doing? What am I doing?" *Scene change music*	(Page 11)
Cue 8	**Tabitha** dials her mobile **Liam**'s *mobile rings*	(Page 13)
Cue 9	**Liam**: "OK then." *Scene change music*	(Page 13)
Cue 10	**Tabitha** exits SR. **Roger** considers what he is doing *Scene change music*	(Page 17)
Cue 11	**Roger**: "Perhaps, Sophie, this evening we could —— " **Roger**'s *mobile rings*	(Page 18)
Cue 12	**Samantha**: "He's late." *Doorbell rings*	(Page 18)
Cue 13	**Tabitha**: "Confidence. After you, Giuseppe." *Scene change music*	(Page 19)
Cue 14	**Tabitha** turns on the hi-fi stereo. She selects a station *Music plays*	(Page 21)
Cue 15	**Liam** turns off the stereo *Music stops*	(Page 21)

Effects Plot

Cue 16	**Tabitha**: "Hmm." *Scene change music*	(Page 23)
Cue 17	**Roger** dials his mobile **Tabitha**'s *other mobile rings*	(Page 25)
Cue 18	**Tabitha**: "OK. New outfit." *Scene change music*	(Page 26)
Cue 19	**Roger**: "Then why wait? Let us kiss, now!" *Doorbell rings*	(Page 29)
Cue 20	**Roger**: " … You fool! You bloody fool!" *Scene change music*	(Page 32)
Cue 21	**Tabitha** hangs up and considers for a few moments *Doorbell rings*	(Page 34)
Cue 22	**Tabitha**: "Come on." *Scene change music*	(Page 36)
Cue 23	**Roger** dials his mobile **Samantha**'s *mobile rings*	(Page 38)
Cue 24	**Roger** and **Samantha** both hang up *Scene change music*	(Page 39)

www.ingramcontent.com/pod-product-compliance
Lightning Source LLC
Chambersburg PA
CBHW070636050426
42450CB00011B/3217